FROM:

Compiled by
Rasheen Hewlett

Illustrated by
Angela Williams

PETER PAUPER PRESS, INC.
WHITE PLAINS, NEW YORK

Designed by Arlene Greco

202 Mamaroneck Avenue
White Plains, NY 10601

ISBN 0-88088-382-0
Printed in China
7 6 5

Visit us at www.peterpauper.com

Pearls of Black Wisdom

I got myself a start by giving myself a start.

Madam C. J. Walker

If you want to accomplish the goals of your life, you have to begin with the spirit.

OPRAH WINFREY

We have learned that our blemishes speak of what all humanity should not do. We understand fully that our glories point to the heights of what human genius can achieve.

NELSON MANDELA

Beauty comes from within. It is sparked by an inner strength and radiance that goes far beyond physical appearance.

JANET JACKSON

Less than one percent of the people in the world reach their full potential—and the reason is they take their focus off what they were doing.

BERRY GORDY, JR.

You ought to believe something in life, believe that thing so fervently that you will stand up with it till the end of your days.

MARTIN LUTHER KING, JR.

I found out life's hard but it ain't impossible.

August Wilson

If you don't have confidence, you'll always find a way not to win.

CARL LEWIS

I've learned that taking charge is a skill, like driving or playing the piano. Each of us, with practice, can learn how to lead.

Judith Jamison

I love myself when I'm laughing.

Zora Neale Hurston

I was determined
to achieve the total
freedom that our history
lessons taught us we were
entitled to, no matter
what the sacrifice.

Rosa Parks

What you do
should have substance
and worth.

Kweisi Mfume

Body and soul,
Black America reveals
the extreme questions
of contemporary life,
questions of freedom
and identity: How can
I be who I am?

JUNE JORDAN

Life owes us nothing.
To have breath and the
ability to think and
create are the gifts.
To speak and see
and move and feel
are extra blessings.

Susan L. Taylor

As you live, believe in life! Always human beings will live and progress to a greater, broader and fuller life. The only possible death is to lose belief in this truth simply because the great end comes slowly, because time is long.

W. E. B. Du Bois

You can't make someone else's choices. You shouldn't let someone else make yours.

COLIN POWELL

If you have no confidence in self you are twice defeated in the race of life. With confidence you have won even before you have started.

MARCUS GARVEY

Rather than trying to balance all of the different aspects of your life, try "blending" them instead.

Bonnie St. John Deane

Ever since our genesis
in the motherland, when
God breathed into our
nostrils and sutured limbs
made from clay, our
spiritual waters have run
still and deep.

CARLYLE FIELDING STEWART III

When you clench your fist, no one can put anything in your hand, nor can your hand pick up anything.

ALEX HALEY

The believer
begins with herself.

Berber proverb

Always be smarter than the people who hire you.

LENA HORNE

We are not fighting for integration, nor are we fighting for separation. We are fighting for recognition as human beings. We are fighting for . . . human rights.

Malcolm X

Though it be a thrilling
and marvelous thing to be
merely young and gifted
in such times, it is doubly
so—doubly dynamic—
to be young, gifted
and black.

LORRAINE HANSBERRY

Everyone and everything around you is your teacher.

KEN KEYES, JR.

To be successful you have to be selfish, or else you never achieve. And once you get to your highest level, then you have to be unselfish. Stay reachable. Stay in touch. Don't isolate.

MICHAEL JORDAN

I started with this idea in my head, "There's two things I've got a right to . . . death or liberty."

Harriet Tubman

We "ourselves"
are high art.

NTOZAKE SHANGE

Being your own man does not mean taking advantage of anyone else.

FLIP WILSON

Can't nothing make your life work if you ain't the architect.

TERRY MCMILLAN

Make peace with the fact that you are human and you are not always going to be able to do everything people will ask of you.

VALERIE FERGUSON

You must not only drive cars, but build them; not only ride planes, but design and fly them.

JESSE JACKSON

It's easy to be independent when you've got money. But to be independent when you haven't got a thing—that's the Lord's test.

MAHALIA JACKSON

Never compromise
who you are personally
to become who you
wish to be
professionally.

Janice Bryant Howroyd

To be a great champion you must believe you are the best. If you're not, pretend you are.

MUHAMMAD ALI

"Divide and conquer" in our world must become "define and empower."

Audre Lorde

I glory in conflict,
that I may hereafter
exult in victory.

FREDERICK DOUGLASS

It is the mind that makes the body.

SOJOURNER TRUTH

I don't know the key to success, but the key to failure is trying to please everybody.

Bill Cosby

The thing I believe. God is inside you and inside everybody else. You come into the world with God.

ALICE WALKER

It's good to have real good people and energy around you to make sure that you stay grounded and to make sure that they keep your ego up and to stay confident and keep your creative juices flowing.

ERYKAH BADU

Full citizenship must be given the colored woman because she needs the ballot for her protection and that of her children.

HALLIE QUINN BROWN

Somehow we must get across to our daughters, sisters and best friends that while being in a relationship can be wonderful and healthy, depending solely on others to define ourselves is limiting and unfulfilling.

CRYSTAL SADLER

To be Black is to shine and aim high.

LEONTYNE PRICE

Let the Afro-American depend on no party, but on himself for his salvation. Let him continue to education, character, and above all, put money in his purse.

IDA B. WELLS

The African race is like a rubber ball; the harder you knock it to the ground, the higher it will rise.

TRADITIONAL SAYING

A man with wisdom is better off than a stupid man with any amount of charm.

African proverb

Black people have been traumatized and psychically wounded. This is something we cannot discuss enough at this historical moment.

BELL HOOKS

We stand on the shoulders of people who died and toiled and sweated so we could have opportunities.

SANDRA DORSEY

Man, if you gotta ask you'll never know.

Louis Armstrong,

when asked to define jazz

Don't hate, it's too big a burden to bear.

MARTIN LUTHER KING, SR.

We are traditionally rather proud of ourselves for having slipped creative work in there between the domestic chores and obligations. I'm not sure we deserve such big A-pluses for all that.

Toni Morrison

I felt that my being an African American was a vital aspect of my leadership; that it provided insights and experiences that I am certain would have been missing had I not been black.

Faye Wattleton

I've discovered that the greatest friends any of us have are knowledge and information.

HARRY BELAFONTE

We can endure,
dream, fail . . . and
still survive.

MAYA ANGELOU

You're either part of the solution or part of the problem.

ELDRIDGE CLEAVER

Faith is the first factor in a life devoted to service. Without faith, nothing is possible. With it, nothing is impossible.

MARY MCLEOD BETHUNE

Nobody will
think you're somebody
if you don't think
so yourself.

African-American expression

The best time to do a thing is when it can be done.

WILLIAM PICKENS

When an old person dies in Africa, it is as though a library had burned.

JESSICA B. HARRIS

Every story I write adds
to me a little, changes
me a little, forces me to
reexamine an attitude or
belief, causes me to
research and learn, helps
me to understand people
and grow. . . . Every story
I create creates me.
I write to create myself.

OCTAVIA E. BUTLER

I have learned that success is to be measured not so much by the position that one has reached in life as by the obstacles which he has overcome while trying to succeed.

BOOKER T. WASHINGTON

The guy who takes a chance, who walks the line between the known and unknown, who is unafraid of failure, will succeed.

GORDON PARKS

Don't be afraid to fail.
Even if you do,
you're bound to learn
something along the way.

Bessie Delany